Keeping Up with Craft Beers

A Journal for Your Tasting Adventures

By Frank Regan

Grandmother's Trunk Press

Published by Grandmother's Trunk Press
specializing in Books to Cultivate Your Enthusiasms

GrandmothersTrunk.com
facebook.com/gtrunkpress

Design and writing © 2016 Grandmother's Trunk

All rights reserved. No part of this book may be reproduced or transmitted in any form or by any means, including but not limited to information storage and retrieval systems, electronic, mechanical, photocopy, recording, etc. without written permission from the copyright holder.

ISBN: 978-0-9967701-0-1

For sales inquiries and special prices for bulk quantities contact us at: office@grandmotherstrunk.com

**DEDICATED
TO
CRAFT BEER
LOVERS
EVERYWHERE**

&

MY IRISH ANCESTORS

LIFE IS SHORT –
DRINK CRAFT BEER!

Table of Contents

Suggestions for use

How to use this journal

Beer List

Beer notes

Lists of Favorite & Least Favorite Beers

Breweries & Brew pubs

Beer Festivals

Websites of interest

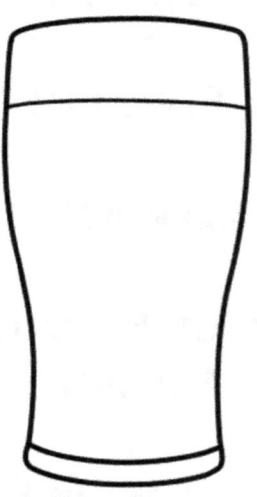

Suggestions for Use:

- Designate certain sections of the book to the breweries or craft beer purveyors you are most likely to patronize. Then it will be easier to find and record all their beer in one section. For example, a brewery you know may have 10 beers regularly. You may want to write them in and check them off as you try them.

- Use a copy of this journal to keep track of each beer you try at a place you frequent that has a large variety on tap.

- Use a separate journal to record beer you sample at beer festivals and then rate the festivals.

- Use an additional journal to record beer you sample at breweries and rate them.

- When ranking, also have a code for where you purchased the beer in case you like the beer, but not the place where you enjoyed it.

- Keep this journal in a designated place so you have easy access and will remember to use it.

- If you forget to bring the journal with you to a beer festival or brewery, use your phone to take photos and keep notes and promptly enter your thoughts when you get home.

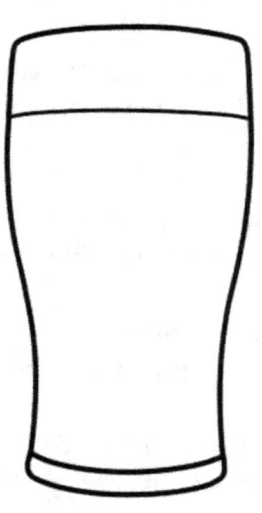

How to Use this Craft Beer Journal

The Beer List

List each beer you try and fill in the "glass" on the left for a basic thumbs up or down. Use a system that makes sense to you. You could just put an "X" for don't bother or a star for good or great. Then, go to the Beer Notes page that corresponds to the number on the right of the beer list to review the brew.

~ Beer Notes Pages ~

You can track each beer you enjoy and those you don't and why. Note your ranking in beer glass in the upper corner for ready reference when you flip through your journal to find your tasting rants and raves. Also use the Beer List to quickly help you find out if you have tried a beer or not and its drinkability.

Lists of Favorites & Least Favorites
Note your top picks & pans here.

Breweries, Brew Pubs, and Festivals

Keep track of where you have your best craft beer drinking experiences on these pages. You can also note those you hear or read about and want to try.

BEER	#
_____	1
_____	2
_____	3
_____	4
_____	5
_____	6
_____	7
_____	8
_____	9
_____	10
_____	11
_____	12
_____	13
_____	14
_____	15

	Beer	**#**
🍺	_____	16
🍺	_____	17
🍺	_____	18
🍺	_____	19
🍺	_____	20
🍺	_____	21
🍺	_____	22
🍺	_____	23
🍺	_____	24
🍺	_____	25
🍺	_____	26
🍺	_____	27
🍺	_____	28
🍺	_____	29
🍺	_____	30

	Beer	**#**
🍺	_____	31
🍺	_____	32
🍺	_____	33
🍺	_____	34
🍺	_____	35
🍺	_____	36
🍺	_____	37
🍺	_____	38
🍺	_____	39
🍺	_____	40
🍺	_____	41
🍺	_____	42
🍺	_____	43
🍺	_____	44
🍺	_____	45

	Beer	**#**
🍺	_____	46
🍺	_____	47
🍺	_____	48
🍺	_____	49
🍺	_____	50
🍺	_____	51
🍺	_____	52
🍺	_____	53
🍺	_____	54
🍺	_____	55
🍺	_____	56
🍺	_____	57
🍺	_____	58
🍺	_____	59
🍺	_____	60

	Beer	**#**
🍺	_____	61
🍺	_____	62
🍺	_____	63
🍺	_____	64
🍺	_____	65
🍺	_____	66
🍺	_____	67
🍺	_____	68
🍺	_____	69
🍺	_____	70
🍺	_____	71
🍺	_____	72
🍺	_____	73
🍺	_____	74
🍺	_____	75

	BEER	**#**
🍺	_____	76
🍺	_____	77
🍺	_____	78
🍺	_____	79
🍺	_____	80
🍺	_____	81
🍺	_____	82
🍺	_____	83
🍺	_____	84
🍺	_____	85
🍺	_____	86
🍺	_____	87
🍺	_____	88
🍺	_____	89
🍺	_____	90

	BEER	#
☐	_____	91
☐	_____	92
☐	_____	93
☐	_____	94
☐	_____	95
☐	_____	96
☐	_____	97
☐	_____	98
☐	_____	99
☐	_____	100

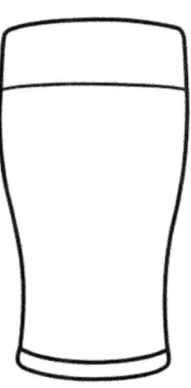

1

Name..
Brewer..
Type/Style..
How Served...
Where Purchased..
Date..................ABV............IBU............Price............
Color...................................Aroma............................
Taste..

What I liked/disliked about this beer:

....
....
....
....
....

Additional notes on body, finish, head, body and mouthfeel:

....
....
....
....
....

Notes on overall experience including how and where served, price, food pairing:

....
....
....
....

2

Name..
Brewer..
Type/Style...
How Served..
Where Purchased...
Date.................ABV..............IBU............Price...............
Color...................................Aroma................................
Taste..

What I liked/disliked about this beer:

....
....
....
....
....

Additional notes on body, finish, head, body and mouthfeel:

....
....
....
....
....

Notes on overall experience including how and where served, price, food pairing:

....
....
....
....

3

Name..
Brewer..
Type/Style...
How Served...
Where Purchased...
Date..................ABV.............IBU............Price.............
Color....................................Aroma................................
Taste..

What I liked/disliked about this beer:

....
....
....
....
....

Additional notes on body, finish, head, body and mouthfeel:

....
....
....
....
....

Notes on overall experience including how and where served, price, food pairing:

....
....
....
....

4

Name..
Brewer..
Type/Style..
How Served...
Where Purchased..
Date..................ABV.............IBU............Price.............
Color......................................Aroma.........................
Taste...

What I liked/disliked about this beer:

....
....
....
....
....

Additional notes on body, finish, head, body and mouthfeel:

....
....
....
....
....

Notes on overall experience including how and where served, price, food pairing:

....
....
....
....

Name..
Brewer..
Type/Style..
How Served..
Where Purchased..
Date.................ABV.............IBU............Price..............
Color....................................Aroma............................
Taste...

What I liked/disliked about this beer:

....
....
....
....
....

Additional notes on body, finish, head, body and mouthfeel:

....
....
....
....
....

Notes on overall experience including how and where served, price, food pairing:

....
....
....
....

6

Name..
Brewer..
Type/Style..
How Served..
Where Purchased..
Date.................ABV.............IBU............Price..............
Color..................................Aroma...........................
Taste...

What I liked/disliked about this beer:

....
....
....
....
....

Additional notes on body, finish, head, body and mouthfeel:

....
....
....
....
....

Notes on overall experience including how and where served, price, food pairing:

....
....
....
....

7

Name..
Brewer..
Type/Style...
How Served..
Where Purchased..
Date.................ABV.............IBU............Price.............
Color..................................Aroma............................
Taste..

What I liked/disliked about this beer:

....
....
....
....
....

Additional notes on body, finish, head, body and mouthfeel:

....
....
....
....
....

Notes on overall experience including how and where served, price, food pairing:

....
....
....
....

8

Name..
Brewer..
Type/Style...
How Served...
Where Purchased..
Date.................ABV.............IBU...........Price...............
Color....................................Aroma................................
Taste...

What I liked/disliked about this beer:

....
....
....
....
....

Additional notes on body, finish, head, body and mouthfeel:

....
....
....
....
....

Notes on overall experience including how and where served, price, food pairing:

....
....
....
....

9

Name..

Brewer..

Type/Style...

How Served...

Where Purchased..

Date..................ABV.............IBU............Price............

Color....................................Aroma..........................

Taste..

What I liked/disliked about this beer:

....
....
....
....
....

Additional notes on body, finish, head, body and mouthfeel:

....
....
....
....
....

Notes on overall experience including how and where served, price, food pairing:

....
....
....
....

10

Name..
Brewer..
Type/Style...
How Served..
Where Purchased..
Date..................ABV.............IBU............Price..............
Color...................................Aroma....................................
Taste...

What I liked/disliked about this beer:

....
....
....
....
....

Additional notes on body, finish, head, body and mouthfeel:

....
....
....
....
....

Notes on overall experience including how and where served, price, food pairing:

....
....
....
....

11

Name..
Brewer..
Type/Style...
How Served..
Where Purchased..
Date................ABV.............IBU............Price............
Color...................................Aroma........................
Taste..

What I liked/disliked about this beer:

....
....
....
....
....

Additional notes on body, finish, head, body and mouthfeel:

....
....
....
....
....

Notes on overall experience including how and where served, price, food pairing:

....
....
....
....

12

Name..
Brewer..
Type/Style...
How Served...
Where Purchased...
Date.................ABV.............IBU............Price...............
Color...Aroma..............................
Taste..

What I liked/disliked about this beer:

....
....
....
....
....

Additional notes on body, finish, head, body and mouthfeel:

....
....
....
....
....

Notes on overall experience including how and where served, price, food pairing:

....
....
....
....

13

Name..
Brewer..
Type/Style..
How Served..
Where Purchased...
Date..................ABV.............IBU............Price.............
Color.............................Aroma...............................
Taste...

What I liked/disliked about this beer:

....
....
....
....
....

Additional notes on body, finish, head, body and mouthfeel:

....
....
....
....
....

Notes on overall experience including how and where served, price, food pairing:

....
....
....
....

|14|

Name..
Brewer..
Type/Style..
How Served..
Where Purchased...
Date.................ABV.............IBU............Price..............
Color..Aroma............................
Taste...

What I liked/disliked about this beer:

....
....
....
....
....

Additional notes on body, finish, head, body and mouthfeel:

....
....
....
....
....

Notes on overall experience including how and where served, price, food pairing:

....
....
....
....

15

Name..
Brewer...
Type/Style..
How Served..
Where Purchased...
Date.................ABV............IBU............Price.............
Color..........................Aroma...........................
Taste...

What I liked/disliked about this beer:

....
....
....
....
....

Additional notes on body, finish, head, body and mouthfeel:

....
....
....
....
....

Notes on overall experience including how and where served, price, food pairing:

....
....
....
....

16

Name..
Brewer..
Type/Style..
How Served...
Where Purchased..
Date..................ABV.............IBU............Price.............
Color...................................Aroma..........................
Taste..

What I liked/disliked about this beer:

....
....
....
....
....

Additional notes on body, finish, head, body and mouthfeel:

....
....
....
....
....

Notes on overall experience including how and where served, price, food pairing:

....
....
....
....

17

Name..

Brewer..

Type/Style...

How Served..

Where Purchased..

Date................ABV............IBU...........Price............

Color..................................Aroma.......................

Taste..

What I liked/disliked about this beer:

....
....
....
....
....

Additional notes on body, finish, head, body and mouthfeel:

....
....
....
....
....

Notes on overall experience including how and where served, price, food pairing:

....
....
....
....

Name..
Brewer..
Type/Style...
How Served..
Where Purchased...
Date.................ABV.............IBU............Price...............
Color.....................................Aroma...............................
Taste...

What I liked/disliked about this beer:

....
....
....
....
....

Additional notes on body, finish, head, body and mouthfeel:

....
....
....
....
....

Notes on overall experience including how and where served, price, food pairing:

....
....
....
....

19

Name..
Brewer..
Type/Style...
How Served...
Where Purchased...
Date..................ABV.............IBU............Price..............
Color...................................Aroma...........................
Taste..

What I liked/disliked about this beer:

....
....
....
....
....

Additional notes on body, finish, head, body and mouthfeel:

....
....
....
....
....

Notes on overall experience including how and where served, price, food pairing:

....
....
....
....

20

Name..
Brewer..
Type/Style...
How Served..
Where Purchased...
Date.................ABV.............IBU............Price...............
Color...................................Aroma............................
Taste...

What I liked/disliked about this beer:

....
....
....
....
....

Additional notes on body, finish, head, body and mouthfeel:

....
....
....
....
....

Notes on overall experience including how and where served, price, food pairing:

....
....
....
....

21

Name..
Brewer..
Type/Style...
How Served..
Where Purchased..
Date.................ABV............IBU............Price.............
Color............................Aroma...........................
Taste..

What I liked/disliked about this beer:

....
....
....
....
....

Additional notes on body, finish, head, body and mouthfeel:

....
....
....
....
....

Notes on overall experience including how and where served, price, food pairing:

....
....
....
....

Name..
Brewer..
Type/Style..
How Served...
Where Purchased...
Date..................ABV.............IBU............Price..............
Color...................................Aroma...............................
Taste...

What I liked/disliked about this beer:

....
....
....
....
....

Additional notes on body, finish, head, body and mouthfeel:

....
....
....
....
....

Notes on overall experience including how and where served, price, food pairing:

....
....
....
....

| 23 |

Name..
Brewer..
Type/Style...
How Served..
Where Purchased..
Date.................ABV.............IBU............Price..............
Color...................................Aroma..................................
Taste..

What I liked/disliked about this beer:

....
....
....
....
....

Additional notes on body, finish, head, body and mouthfeel:

....
....
....
....
....

Notes on overall experience including how and where served, price, food pairing:

....
....
....
....

| 24 |

Name..
Brewer..
Type/Style...
How Served...
Where Purchased..
Date................ABV.............IBU............Price...............
Color..Aroma............................
Taste..

What I liked/disliked about this beer:

....
....
....
....
....

Additional notes on body, finish, head, body and mouthfeel:

....
....
....
....
....

Notes on overall experience including how and where served, price, food pairing:

....
....
....
....

Name..
Brewer..
Type/Style..
How Served...
Where Purchased...
Date..................ABV.............IBU............Price..............
Color.............................Aroma.............................
Taste...

What I liked/disliked about this beer:

....
....
....
....
....

Additional notes on body, finish, head, body and mouthfeel:

....
....
....
....
....

Notes on overall experience including how and where served, price, food pairing:

....
....
....
....

Name..
Brewer..
Type/Style...
How Served..
Where Purchased..
Date.................ABV.............IBU............Price...............
Color...................................Aroma................................
Taste..

What I liked/disliked about this beer:

....
....
....
....
....

Additional notes on body, finish, head, body and mouthfeel:

....
....
....
....
....

Notes on overall experience including how and where served, price, food pairing:

....
....
....
....

27

Name..
Brewer..
Type/Style...
How Served..
Where Purchased...
Date..................ABV.............IBU............Price.............
Color...................................Aroma...........................
Taste..

What I liked/disliked about this beer:

....
....
....
....
....

Additional notes on body, finish, head, body and mouthfeel:

....
....
....
....
....

Notes on overall experience including how and where served, price, food pairing:

....
....
....
....

28

Name..
Brewer..
Type/Style...
How Served..
Where Purchased...
Date.................ABV.............IBU............Price..............
Color....................................Aroma................................
Taste..

What I liked/disliked about this beer:

....
....
....
....
....

Additional notes on body, finish, head, body and mouthfeel:

....
....
....
....
....

Notes on overall experience including how and where served, price, food pairing:

....
....
....
....

[29]

Name..
Brewer..
Type/Style...
How Served...
Where Purchased...
Date..................ABV.............IBU............Price...............
Color....................................Aroma...................................
Taste..

What I liked/disliked about this beer:

....
....
....
....
....

Additional notes on body, finish, head, body and mouthfeel:

....
....
....
....
....

Notes on overall experience including how and where served, price, food pairing:

....
....
....
....

30

Name..
Brewer..
Type/Style...
How Served..
Where Purchased..
Date.................ABV.............IBU............Price...............
Color.....................................Aroma...............................
Taste..

What I liked/disliked about this beer:

....
....
....
....
....

Additional notes on body, finish, head, body and mouthfeel:

....
....
....
....
....

Notes on overall experience including how and where served, price, food pairing:

....
....
....
....

31

Name..
Brewer..
Type/Style...
How Served...
Where Purchased...
Date..................ABV.............IBU............Price..............
Color..................................Aroma...............................
Taste..

What I liked/disliked about this beer:

....
....
....
....
....

Additional notes on body, finish, head, body and mouthfeel:

....
....
....
....
....

Notes on overall experience including how and where served, price, food pairing:

....
....
....
....

32

Name..
Brewer..
Type/Style...
How Served...
Where Purchased..
Date.................ABV............IBU............Price..............
Color...................................Aroma..............................
Taste..

What I liked/disliked about this beer:

....
....
....
....
....

Additional notes on body, finish, head, body and mouthfeel:

....
....
....
....
....

Notes on overall experience including how and where served, price, food pairing:

....
....
....
....

33

Name..
Brewer..
Type/Style..
How Served..
Where Purchased..
Date..................ABV.............IBU............Price..............
Color....................................Aroma............................
Taste..

What I liked/disliked about this beer:

....
....
....
....
....

Additional notes on body, finish, head, body and mouthfeel:

....
....
....
....
....

Notes on overall experience including how and where served, price, food pairing:

....
....
....
....

Name..
Brewer..
Type/Style..
How Served...
Where Purchased..
Date..................ABV.............IBU............Price.............
Color....................................Aroma..............................
Taste..

What I liked/disliked about this beer:

....
....
....
....
....

Additional notes on body, finish, head, body and mouthfeel:

....
....
....
....
....

Notes on overall experience including how and where served, price, food pairing:

....
....
....
....

35

Name..
Brewer..
Type/Style..
How Served...
Where Purchased...
Date................ABV.............IBU............Price............
Color...................................Aroma.........................
Taste...

What I liked/disliked about this beer:

....
....
....
....
....

Additional notes on body, finish, head, body and mouthfeel:

....
....
....
....
....

Notes on overall experience including how and where served, price, food pairing:

....
....
....
....

Name..
Brewer..
Type/Style...
How Served...
Where Purchased..
Date.................ABV.............IBU............Price..............
Color...................................Aroma............................
Taste..

What I liked/disliked about this beer:

....
....
....
....
....

Additional notes on body, finish, head, body and mouthfeel:

....
....
....
....
....

Notes on overall experience including how and where served, price, food pairing:

....
....
....
....

37

Name..
Brewer..
Type/Style..
How Served..
Where Purchased..
Date.................ABV............IBU............Price............
Color..................................Aroma............................
Taste..

What I liked/disliked about this beer:

....
....
....
....
....

Additional notes on body, finish, head, body and mouthfeel:

....
....
....
....
....

Notes on overall experience including how and where served, price, food pairing:

....
....
....
....

Name..
Brewer..
Type/Style...
How Served..
Where Purchased..
Date.................ABV.............IBU............Price...............
Color...................................Aroma................................
Taste..

What I liked/disliked about this beer:

....
....
....
....
....

Additional notes on body, finish, head, body and mouthfeel:

....
....
....
....
....

Notes on overall experience including how and where served, price, food pairing:

....
....
....
....

39

Name..
Brewer..
Type/Style..
How Served...
Where Purchased...
Date..................ABV.............IBU............Price.............
Color...................................Aroma..........................
Taste...

What I liked/disliked about this beer:

....
....
....
....
....

Additional notes on body, finish, head, body and mouthfeel:

....
....
....
....
....

Notes on overall experience including how and where served, price, food pairing:

....
....
....
....

40

Name..
Brewer..
Type/Style...
How Served..
Where Purchased..
Date.................ABV.............IBU............Price..............
Color...................................Aroma................................
Taste...

What I liked/disliked about this beer:

....
....
....
....
....

Additional notes on body, finish, head, body and mouthfeel:

....
....
....
....
....

Notes on overall experience including how and where served, price, food pairing:

....
....
....
....

41

Name..
Brewer..
Type/Style..
How Served..
Where Purchased..
Date.................ABV.............IBU............Price.............
Color...................................Aroma...........................
Taste..

What I liked/disliked about this beer:

....
....
....
....
....

Additional notes on body, finish, head, body and mouthfeel:

....
....
....
....
....

Notes on overall experience including how and where served, price, food pairing:

....
....
....
....

Name..
Brewer..
Type/Style...
How Served...
Where Purchased..
Date.................ABV.............IBU............Price..............
Color...................................Aroma............................
Taste..

What I liked/disliked about this beer:

....
....
....
....
....

Additional notes on body, finish, head, body and mouthfeel:

....
....
....
....
....

Notes on overall experience including how and where served, price, food pairing:

....
....
....
....

| 43 |

Name..
Brewer..
Type/Style...
How Served...
Where Purchased...
Date..................ABV.............IBU............Price.............
Color...................................Aroma.................................
Taste...

What I liked/disliked about this beer:

....
....
....
....

Additional notes on body, finish, head, body and mouthfeel:

....
....
....
....

Notes on overall experience including how and where served, price, food pairing:

....
....
....
....

Name..
Brewer..
Type/Style...
How Served..
Where Purchased..
Date.................ABV.............IBU............Price...............
Color....................................Aroma............................
Taste..

What I liked/disliked about this beer:

....
....
....
....
....

Additional notes on body, finish, head, body and mouthfeel:

....
....
....
....
....

Notes on overall experience including how and where served, price, food pairing:

....
....
....
....

45

Name..
Brewer..
Type/Style...
How Served..
Where Purchased..
Date..................ABV.............IBU.............Price..............
Color...................................Aroma...............................
Taste..

What I liked/disliked about this beer:

....
....
....
....
....

Additional notes on body, finish, head, body and mouthfeel:

....
....
....
....
....

Notes on overall experience including how and where served, price, food pairing:

....
....
....
....

Name..
Brewer..
Type/Style...
How Served..
Where Purchased...
Date.................ABV.............IBU............Price.............
Color....................................Aroma...........................
Taste...

What I liked/disliked about this beer:

....
....
....
....
....

Additional notes on body, finish, head, body and mouthfeel:

....
....
....
....
....

Notes on overall experience including how and where served, price, food pairing:

....
....
....
....

Name..
Brewer..
Type/Style..
How Served..
Where Purchased..
Date..................ABV..............IBU............Price..............
Color.....................................Aroma............................
Taste...

What I liked/disliked about this beer:

....
....
....
....
....

Additional notes on body, finish, head, body and mouthfeel:

....
....
....
....
....

Notes on overall experience including how and where served, price, food pairing:

....
....
....
....

48

Name..
Brewer..
Type/Style..
How Served...
Where Purchased...
Date.................ABV.............IBU............Price...............
Color....................................Aroma............................
Taste..

What I liked/disliked about this beer:

....
....
....
....
....

Additional notes on body, finish, head, body and mouthfeel:

....
....
....
....
....

Notes on overall experience including how and where served, price, food pairing:

....
....
....
....

49

Name..
Brewer..
Type/Style..
How Served..
Where Purchased..
Date..................ABV............IBU............Price..............
Color...................................Aroma..............................
Taste..

What I liked/disliked about this beer:

....
....
....
....
....

Additional notes on body, finish, head, body and mouthfeel:

....
....
....
....
....

Notes on overall experience including how and where served, price, food pairing:

....
....
....
....

50

Name..
Brewer..
Type/Style...
How Served...
Where Purchased...
Date................ABV.............IBU............Price..............
Color....................................Aroma.............................
Taste...

What I liked/disliked about this beer:

....
....
....
....
....

Additional notes on body, finish, head, body and mouthfeel:

....
....
....
....
....

Notes on overall experience including how and where served, price, food pairing:

....
....
....
....

51

Name..
Brewer...
Type/Style...
How Served...
Where Purchased...
Date................ABV............IBU............Price............
Color.................................Aroma....................
Taste..

What I liked/disliked about this beer:

....
....
....
....
....

Additional notes on body, finish, head, body and mouthfeel:

....
....
....
....
....

Notes on overall experience including how and where served, price, food pairing:

....
....
....
....

52

Name..
Brewer..
Type/Style..
How Served...
Where Purchased...
Date..................ABV.............IBU............Price..............
Color....................................Aroma................................
Taste...

What I liked/disliked about this beer:

....
....
....
....
....

Additional notes on body, finish, head, body and mouthfeel:

....
....
....
....
....

Notes on overall experience including how and where served, price, food pairing:

....
....
....
....

53

Name...
Brewer...
Type/Style...
How Served..
Where Purchased...
Date.................ABV.............IBU............Price..............
Color...................................Aroma.................................
Taste..

What I liked/disliked about this beer:

....
....
....
....
....

Additional notes on body, finish, head, body and mouthfeel:

....
....
....
....
....

Notes on overall experience including how and where served, price, food pairing:

....
....
....
....

54

Name..
Brewer..
Type/Style...
How Served..
Where Purchased...
Date.................ABV.............IBU............Price...............
Color..................................Aroma...............................
Taste...

What I liked/disliked about this beer:

....
....
....
....
....

Additional notes on body, finish, head, body and mouthfeel:

....
....
....
....
....

Notes on overall experience including how and where served, price, food pairing:

....
....
....
....

55

Name..
Brewer..
Type/Style...
How Served..
Where Purchased...
Date.................ABV............IBU............Price.............
Color...................................Aroma.............................
Taste..

What I liked/disliked about this beer:

....
....
....
....
....

Additional notes on body, finish, head, body and mouthfeel:

....
....
....
....
....

Notes on overall experience including how and where served, price, food pairing:

....
....
....
....

Name..
Brewer..
Type/Style...
How Served..
Where Purchased..
Date.................ABV.............IBU............Price...............
Color...................................Aroma...............................
Taste..

What I liked/disliked about this beer:

....
....
....
....
....

Additional notes on body, finish, head, body and mouthfeel:

....
....
....
....
....

Notes on overall experience including how and where served, price, food pairing:

....
....
....
....

57

Name..
Brewer..
Type/Style...
How Served..
Where Purchased..
Date..................ABV.............IBU.............Price..............
Color...................................Aroma...............................
Taste..

What I liked/disliked about this beer:

....
....
....
....
....

Additional notes on body, finish, head, body and mouthfeel:

....
....
....
....
....

Notes on overall experience including how and where served, price, food pairing:

....
....
....
....

58

Name..
Brewer..
Type/Style...
How Served..
Where Purchased..
Date..................ABV.............IBU............Price..............
Color...................................Aroma...............................
Taste..

What I liked/disliked about this beer:

....
....
....
....
....

Additional notes on body, finish, head, body and mouthfeel:

....
....
....
....
....

Notes on overall experience including how and where served, price, food pairing:

....
....
....
....

59

Name..

Brewer..

Type/Style..

How Served...

Where Purchased..

Date.................ABV.............IBU............Price............

Color...................................Aroma............................

Taste...

What I liked/disliked about this beer:

....
....
....
....
....

Additional notes on body, finish, head, body and mouthfeel:

....
....
....
....
....

Notes on overall experience including how and where served, price, food pairing:

....
....
....
....

Name..
Brewer..
Type/Style...
How Served..
Where Purchased..
Date.................ABV.............IBU............Price...............
Color...................................Aroma...........................
Taste...

What I liked/disliked about this beer:

....
....
....
....
....

Additional notes on body, finish, head, body and mouthfeel:

....
....
....
....
....

Notes on overall experience including how and where served, price, food pairing:

....
....
....
....

61

Name..
Brewer..
Type/Style..
How Served...
Where Purchased..
Date.................ABV............IBU............Price............
Color...................................Aroma...........................
Taste..

What I liked/disliked about this beer:

....
....
....
....
....

Additional notes on body, finish, head, body and mouthfeel:

....
....
....
....
....

Notes on overall experience including how and where served, price, food pairing:

....
....
....
....

Name..
Brewer..
Type/Style..
How Served..
Where Purchased..
Date.................ABV.............IBU............Price...............
Color...............................Aroma...........................
Taste...

What I liked/disliked about this beer:

....
....
....
....
....

Additional notes on body, finish, head, body and mouthfeel:

....
....
....
....
....

Notes on overall experience including how and where served, price, food pairing:

....
....
....
....

63

Name..
Brewer..
Type/Style..
How Served..
Where Purchased..
Date..................ABV.............IBU............Price............
Color...................................Aroma..................
Taste...

What I liked/disliked about this beer:

....
....
....
....
....

Additional notes on body, finish, head, body and mouthfeel:

....
....
....
....
....

Notes on overall experience including how and where served, price, food pairing:

....
....
....
....

Name..
Brewer..
Type/Style...
How Served...
Where Purchased..
Date.................ABV............IBU............Price..............
Color...Aroma..........................
Taste...

What I liked/disliked about this beer:

....
....
....
....
....

Additional notes on body, finish, head, body and mouthfeel:

....
....
....
....
....

Notes on overall experience including how and where served, price, food pairing:

....
....
....
....

Name..
Brewer..
Type/Style...
How Served...
Where Purchased..
Date.................ABV.............IBU............Price..............
Color...................................Aroma................................
Taste...

What I liked/disliked about this beer:

....
....
....
....
....

Additional notes on body, finish, head, body and mouthfeel:

....
....
....
....
....

Notes on overall experience including how and where served, price, food pairing:

....
....
....
....

Name..

Brewer..

Type/Style...

How Served...

Where Purchased..

Date.................ABV.............IBU............Price...............

Color...................................Aroma............................

Taste...

What I liked/disliked about this beer:

....
....
....
....
....

Additional notes on body, finish, head, body and mouthfeel:

....
....
....
....
....

Notes on overall experience including how and where served, price, food pairing:

....
....
....
....

67

Name..
Brewer..
Type/Style...
How Served..
Where Purchased...
Date..................ABV.............IBU............Price.............
Color...................................Aroma..................................
Taste..

What I liked/disliked about this beer:

....
....
....
....
....

Additional notes on body, finish, head, body and mouthfeel:

....
....
....
....
....

Notes on overall experience including how and where served, price, food pairing:

....
....
....
....

68

Name..
Brewer..
Type/Style...
How Served..
Where Purchased..
Date................ABV.............IBU............Price...............
Color...................................Aroma...........................
Taste..

What I liked/disliked about this beer:

....
....
....
....
....

Additional notes on body, finish, head, body and mouthfeel:

....
....
....
....
....

Notes on overall experience including how and where served, price, food pairing:

....
....
....
....

Name..
Brewer..
Type/Style...
How Served...
Where Purchased..
Date.................ABV............IBU............Price.............
Color..................................Aroma............................
Taste..

What I liked/disliked about this beer:

....
....
....
....
....

Additional notes on body, finish, head, body and mouthfeel:

....
....
....
....
....

Notes on overall experience including how and where served, price, food pairing:

....
....
....
....

|70|

Name..
Brewer..
Type/Style..
How Served...
Where Purchased...
Date.................ABV............IBU............Price.............
Color...................................Aroma................................
Taste..

What I liked/disliked about this beer:

....
....
....
....
....

Additional notes on body, finish, head, body and mouthfeel:

....
....
....
....
....

Notes on overall experience including how and where served, price, food pairing:

....
....
....
....

71

Name..
Brewer...
Type/Style..
How Served...
Where Purchased..
Date..................ABV.............IBU............Price............
Color..................................Aroma...............................
Taste...

What I liked/disliked about this beer:

....
....
....
....
....

Additional notes on body, finish, head, body and mouthfeel:

....
....
....
....
....

Notes on overall experience including how and where served, price, food pairing:

....
....
....
....

Name..
Brewer..
Type/Style...
How Served...
Where Purchased..
Date.................ABV.............IBU............Price...............
Color....................................Aroma...............................
Taste..

What I liked/disliked about this beer:

....
....
....
....
....

Additional notes on body, finish, head, body and mouthfeel:

....
....
....
....
....

Notes on overall experience including how and where served, price, food pairing:

....
....
....
....

73

Name..
Brewer..
Type/Style..
How Served...
Where Purchased..
Date..................ABV.............IBU............Price..............
Color....................................Aroma...............................
Taste..

What I liked/disliked about this beer:

....
....
....
....
....

Additional notes on body, finish, head, body and mouthfeel:

....
....
....
....
....

Notes on overall experience including how and where served, price, food pairing:

....
....
....
....

74

Name..
Brewer..
Type/Style..
How Served..
Where Purchased...
Date.................ABV.............IBU............Price..............
Color.................................Aroma...........................
Taste..

What I liked/disliked about this beer:

....
....
....
....
....

Additional notes on body, finish, head, body and mouthfeel:

....
....
....
....
....

Notes on overall experience including how and where served, price, food pairing:

....
....
....
....

75

Name..
Brewer..
Type/Style..
How Served..
Where Purchased..
Date..................ABV.............IBU............Price..............
Color....................................Aroma...............................
Taste..

What I liked/disliked about this beer:

....
....
....
....
....

Additional notes on body, finish, head, body and mouthfeel:

....
....
....
....
....

Notes on overall experience including how and where served, price, food pairing:

....
....
....
....

76

Name..
Brewer..
Type/Style...
How Served..
Where Purchased..
Date.................ABV.............IBU............Price.............
Color....................................Aroma............................
Taste...

What I liked/disliked about this beer:

....
....
....
....
....

Additional notes on body, finish, head, body and mouthfeel:

....
....
....
....
....

Notes on overall experience including how and where served, price, food pairing:

....
....
....
....

| 77 |

Name..
Brewer..
Type/Style...
How Served..
Where Purchased..
Date..................ABV..............IBU............Price..............
Color...................................Aroma............................
Taste..

What I liked/disliked about this beer:

....
....
....
....
....

Additional notes on body, finish, head, body and mouthfeel:

....
....
....
....
....

Notes on overall experience including how and where served, price, food pairing:

....
....
....
....

Name..
Brewer..
Type/Style..
How Served...
Where Purchased...
Date.................ABV.............IBU.............Price...............
Color..................................Aroma................................
Taste..

What I liked/disliked about this beer:

....
....
....
....
....

Additional notes on body, finish, head, body and mouthfeel:

....
....
....
....
....

Notes on overall experience including how and where served, price, food pairing:

....
....
....
....

79

Name..
Brewer..
Type/Style..
How Served..
Where Purchased..
Date.................ABV............IBU............Price.............
Color..................................Aroma..............................
Taste..

What I liked/disliked about this beer:

....
....
....
....

Additional notes on body, finish, head, body and mouthfeel:

....
....
....
....
....

Notes on overall experience including how and where served, price, food pairing:

....
....
....
....

80

Name..
Brewer..
Type/Style...
How Served...
Where Purchased...
Date................ABV.............IBU............Price...............
Color...............................Aroma...............................
Taste..

What I liked/disliked about this beer:

....
....
....
....
....

Additional notes on body, finish, head, body and mouthfeel:

....
....
....
....
....

Notes on overall experience including how and where served, price, food pairing:

....
....
....
....

Name..
Brewer..
Type/Style..
How Served..
Where Purchased...
Date..................ABV.............IBU............Price..............
Color...................................Aroma................................
Taste..

What I liked/disliked about this beer:

....
....
....
....
....

Additional notes on body, finish, head, body and mouthfeel:

....
....
....
....
....

Notes on overall experience including how and where served, price, food pairing:

....
....
....
....

Name..
Brewer..
Type/Style...
How Served..
Where Purchased...
Date..................ABV.............IBU............Price..............
Color....................................Aroma................................
Taste..

What I liked/disliked about this beer:

....
....
....
....
....

Additional notes on body, finish, head, body and mouthfeel:

....
....
....
....
....

Notes on overall experience including how and where served, price, food pairing:

....
....
....
....

83

Name..
Brewer..
Type/Style..
How Served...
Where Purchased...
Date..................ABV.............IBU............Price..............
Color...................................Aroma..............................
Taste...

What I liked/disliked about this beer:

....
....
....
....
....

Additional notes on body, finish, head, body and mouthfeel:

....
....
....
....
....

Notes on overall experience including how and where served, price, food pairing:

....
....
....
....

Name..
Brewer..
Type/Style...
How Served..
Where Purchased...
Date..................ABV.............IBU............Price...............
Color.................................Aroma.............................
Taste...

What I liked/disliked about this beer:

....
....
....
....
....

Additional notes on body, finish, head, body and mouthfeel:

....
....
....
....
....

Notes on overall experience including how and where served, price, food pairing:

....
....
....
....

85

Name..
Brewer..
Type/Style..
How Served..
Where Purchased...
Date..................ABV.............IBU............Price..............
Color....................................Aroma.............................
Taste...

What I liked/disliked about this beer:

....
....
....
....
....

Additional notes on body, finish, head, body and mouthfeel:

....
....
....
....
....

Notes on overall experience including how and where served, price, food pairing:

....
....
....
....

Name..
Brewer..
Type/Style..
How Served..
Where Purchased...
Date.................ABV.............IBU............Price...............
Color...............................Aroma.................................
Taste...

What I liked/disliked about this beer:

....
....
....
....
....

Additional notes on body, finish, head, body and mouthfeel:

....
....
....
....
....

Notes on overall experience including how and where served, price, food pairing:

....
....
....
....

Name..
Brewer..
Type/Style..
How Served...
Where Purchased..
Date.................ABV............IBU............Price.............
Color................................Aroma...........................
Taste..

What I liked/disliked about this beer:

....
....
....
....
....

Additional notes on body, finish, head, body and mouthfeel:

....
....
....
....
....

Notes on overall experience including how and where served, price, food pairing:

....
....
....
....

88

Name..
Brewer..
Type/Style..
How Served..
Where Purchased..
Date.................ABV............IBU...........Price..............
Color...................................Aroma..........................
Taste...

What I liked/disliked about this beer:

....
....
....
....
....

Additional notes on body, finish, head, body and mouthfeel:

....
....
....
....
....

Notes on overall experience including how and where served, price, food pairing:

....
....
....
....

89

Name..
Brewer..
Type/Style...
How Served...
Where Purchased...
Date.................ABV.............IBU............Price.............
Color...................................Aroma...............................
Taste...

What I liked/disliked about this beer:

....
....
....
....
....

Additional notes on body, finish, head, body and mouthfeel:

....
....
....
....
....

Notes on overall experience including how and where served, price, food pairing:

....
....
....
....

90

Name..
Brewer..
Type/Style..
How Served..
Where Purchased..
Date.................ABV.............IBU............Price...............
Color.................................Aroma................................
Taste..

What I liked/disliked about this beer:

....
....
....
....
....

Additional notes on body, finish, head, body and mouthfeel:

....
....
....
....
....

Notes on overall experience including how and where served, price, food pairing:

....
....
....
....

91

Name..
Brewer...
Type/Style..
How Served..
Where Purchased...
Date.................ABV............IBU............Price.............
Color...................................Aroma........................
Taste...

What I liked/disliked about this beer:

....
....
....
....
....

Additional notes on body, finish, head, body and mouthfeel:

....
....
....
....
....

Notes on overall experience including how and where served, price, food pairing:

....
....
....
....

Name..
Brewer..
Type/Style..
How Served..
Where Purchased..
Date..................ABV.............IBU............Price...............
Color...........................Aroma.................................
Taste...

What I liked/disliked about this beer:

....
....
....
....
....

Additional notes on body, finish, head, body and mouthfeel:

....
....
....
....
....

Notes on overall experience including how and where served, price, food pairing:

....
....
....
....

93

Name..
Brewer..
Type/Style..
How Served..
Where Purchased..
Date..................ABV............IBU............Price.............
Color....................................Aroma...............................
Taste..

What I liked/disliked about this beer:

....
....
....
....
....

Additional notes on body, finish, head, body and mouthfeel:

....
....
....
....
....

Notes on overall experience including how and where served, price, food pairing:

....
....
....
....

Name..
Brewer..
Type/Style..
How Served...
Where Purchased...
Date.................ABV.............IBU............Price..............
Color....................................Aroma....................
Taste...

What I liked/disliked about this beer:

....
....
....
....
....

Additional notes on body, finish, head, body and mouthfeel:

....
....
....
....
....

Notes on overall experience including how and where served, price, food pairing:

....
....
....
....

95

Name..
Brewer..
Type/Style..
How Served...
Where Purchased...
Date..................ABV.............IBU............Price...............
Color...................................Aroma................................
Taste...

What I liked/disliked about this beer:

....
....
....
....
....

Additional notes on body, finish, head, body and mouthfeel:

....
....
....
....
....

Notes on overall experience including how and where served, price, food pairing:

....
....
....
....

96

Name..
Brewer..
Type/Style..
How Served..
Where Purchased..
Date..................ABV.............IBU............Price...............
Color.....................................Aroma..............................
Taste...

What I liked/disliked about this beer:

....
....
....
....
....

Additional notes on body, finish, head, body and mouthfeel:

....
....
....
....
....

Notes on overall experience including how and where served, price, food pairing:

....
....
....
....

97

Name..
Brewer..
Type/Style...
How Served..
Where Purchased..
Date..................ABV.............IBU.............Price..............
Color....................................Aroma...............................
Taste..

What I liked/disliked about this beer:

....
....
....
....
....

Additional notes on body, finish, head, body and mouthfeel:

....
....
....
....
....

Notes on overall experience including how and where served, price, food pairing:

....
....
....
....

Name..
Brewer..
Type/Style...
How Served..
Where Purchased..
Date................ABV............IBU............Price...............
Color.................................Aroma...............................
Taste...

What I liked/disliked about this beer:

....
....
....
....
....

Additional notes on body, finish, head, body and mouthfeel:

....
....
....
....
....

Notes on overall experience including how and where served, price, food pairing:

....
....
....
....

99

Name..
Brewer..
Type/Style..
How Served..
Where Purchased..
Date.................ABV.............IBU............Price.............
Color...............................Aroma...........................
Taste..

What I liked/disliked about this beer:

....
....
....
....
....

Additional notes on body, finish, head, body and mouthfeel:

....
....
....
....
....

Notes on overall experience including how and where served, price, food pairing:

....
....
....
....

100

Name..
Brewer..
Type/Style...
How Served..
Where Purchased...
Date.................ABV.............IBU...........Price..............
Color...................................Aroma................................
Taste...

What I liked/disliked about this beer:

....
....
....
....
....

Additional notes on body, finish, head, body and mouthfeel:

....
....
....
....
....

Notes on overall experience including how and where served, price, food pairing:

....
....
....
....

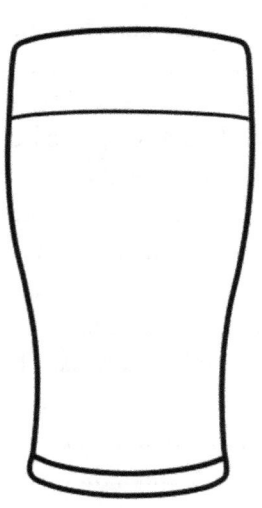

FAVORITE BEERS

Here you can list your top picks from
all the beers you have been tasting.

BEER #	NAME

LEAST FAVORITE

Here you can list those that you gave a thumbs down to.

BEER #	NAME

BREWERIES & BREWPUBS I LIKE
(or would like to visit.)

Name: ....
Town: ....
Notes: ....
....

Name: ....
Town: ....
Notes: ....
....

Name: ....
Town: ....
Notes: ....
....

Name: ....
Town: ....
Notes: ....
....

Name: ....
Town: ....
Notes: ....
....

Name: ....
Town: ....
Notes: ....
....

Name: ....
Town: ....
Notes: ....
....

Breweries & Brewpubs I Like
(or would like to visit.)

Name: ....
Town: ....
Notes: ....
....

Name: ....
Town: ....
Notes: ....
....

Name: ....
Town: ....
Notes: ....
....

Name: ....
Town: ....
Notes: ....
....

Name: ....
Town: ....
Notes: ....
....

Name: ....
Town: ....
Notes: ....
....

Name: ....
Town: ....
Notes: ....
....

BREWERIES & BREWPUBS I LIKE
(or would like to visit.)

Name: ....
Town: ....
Notes: ....
....

Name: ....
Town: ....
Notes: ....
....

Name: ....
Town: ....
Notes: ....
....

Name: ....
Town: ....
Notes: ....
....

Name: ....
Town: ....
Notes: ....
....

Name: ....
Town: ....
Notes: ....
....

Name: ....
Town: ....
Notes: ....
....

Name: ....
Town: ....
Notes: ....
....

BEER FESTIVAL NOTES

Name: ....
Place: ....
Notes: ....
....

Name: ....
Place: ....
Notes: ....
....

Name: ....
Place: ....
Notes: ....
....

Name: ....
Place: ....
Notes: ....
....

Name: ....
Place: ....
Notes: ....
....

Name: ....
Place: ....
Notes: ....
....

Name: ....
Place: ....
Notes: ....

BEER FESTIVAL NOTES

Name: ....
Place: ....
Notes: ....
....

Name: ....
Place: ....
Notes: ....
....

Name: ....
Place: ....
Notes: ....
....

Name: ....
Place: ....
Notes: ....
....

Name: ....
Place: ....
Notes: ....
....

Name: ....
Place: ....
Notes: ....
....

Name: ....
Place: ....
Notes: ....

Websites about craft beer that you might enjoy:

alestreetnews.com
beeradvocate.com
beerwikia.com
brewingnews.com
brewsassociation.org
craftbeer.com
cicerone.org
draftmag.com
growlermag.com
pubcrawler.com

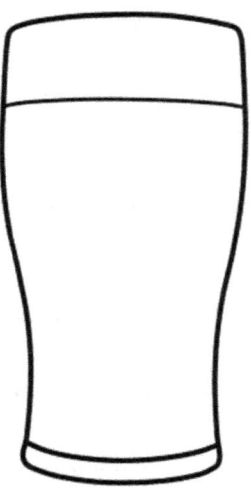

ABOUT THIS BOOK:

A beer festival on Sebago Lake in Maine about seven years ago was the beginning of an awakening of an interest in exploring craft beer. A local brew pub and a pub a few towns over with about 80 beers on tap upped the opportunities and variety to sample. Breweries popping up in and around the hometown as well as in a favorite Maine destination offered more and more tempting brews. The increasing choices and variety with clever and sometimes similar names made it hard to keep track of the delights and disappointments found on tap and in stores. As a result, this journal was created to not only list beers tried, but also to keep track of which ones earned raves and which ones rants and why.

ABOUT THE PUBLISHER:

Grandmother's Trunk Press has been publishing custom guides, newsletters, and short run booklets and books since 1974. This journal is one in a series planned for wider distribution online and in stores.

The book, *A Woman's Ways & Means: Making It Happen, 24 Wild Years in the Massachusetts House* by Barbara E. Gray with Debra Regan Cleveland, was published under our imprint Drummer Cove Publications and limited quantities are available through MassBayTrading.com or GrandmothersTrunk.com.

www.ingramcontent.com/pod-product-compliance
Lightning Source LLC
Chambersburg PA
CBHW070628300426
44113CB00010B/1700